IT MIGHT BE A
RED FLAG IF...

IT MIGHT BE A
RED FLAG IF...

A Humorous and Inspirational
Guide to Dating

BY JENNIFER LOPEZ

ARCHWAY
PUBLISHING

Archway Publishing books may be ordered through booksellers or by contacting:

Archway Publishing
1663 Liberty Drive
Bloomington, IN 47403
www.archwaypublishing.com
1-(888)-242-5904

ISBN: 978-1-4808-1434-9 (sc)
ISBN: 978-1-4808-1435-6 (e)

Library of Congress Control Number: 2014922632

Printed in the United States of America.

Archway Publishing rev. date: 12/19/2014

TO MYSELF,
TEN YEARS AGO

INTRODUCTION

I decided to write this book after being single for more than ten years, and after breakups or bad dates, I always found myself saying, "I ignored the red flags."

Most of these red flags I have personally experienced. Some are humorous and some are serious signs that may save a heart, bank account, liver, marriage, or even a life. I have been lucky to get away with only a broken heart, some debt, and maybe a broken door or two. Other women have not been so lucky. If we fail to see warning signs, life can change in an instant.

I also want to help women get past red flags and figure out why we let ourselves get hurt or stay with men who are abusive or not right for us. Breaking up is hard, and I now know why a lot of break-up songs are so popular. Take for instance Carrie Underwood's "Before He Cheats."

I know many of us have thought about taking a baseball bat to his precious truck or letting our keys create some impressive artwork, but where would that leave us besides in jail? Speaking of jail, when you commit a crime, you get your Miranda rights read to you. Remember the part that says, "If you can't afford an attorney, one will be appointed to you"? That's for *free*! When we get our hearts broken, why can't someone approach us and say, "If you can't afford a shrink, one will be appointed to you for *free*—but wait! If you call within the next thirty minutes, you will also receive a year's supply of wine and chocolate!"

Now, I have felt the satisfaction of flinging a framed picture off a balcony. Just make sure your kids aren't watching and the neighbor's cat is out of the way.

This book was written in the hope of giving women out there like me some help in finding true love. I started writing a book at the age of fourteen. Who would have thought that life would continue to present me with trials and entertainment that I would actually write a non-fiction book twenty-eight years later? I thought about writing a song but then realized radio stations won't play a thirty-two-minute-long song.

This book is not intended to offend men; in fact, it applies to all sexes. However, the last time I checked I was a woman, so it is written from a woman's point of view.

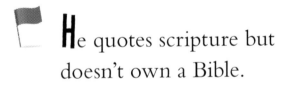 He erases all texts from his female friends.

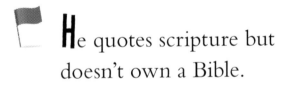 He quotes scripture but doesn't own a Bible.

You find a hidden bag of pills, and he tells you they're aspirin.

He has a female-name tattoo, and it's not *Mom*.

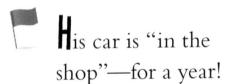 **H**is nickname refers to a certain body part of his.

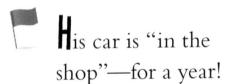 **H**is car is "in the shop"—for a year!

He can only call you;
you can't call him.

Every female friend on his
Facebook page is a "cousin."

He is willing to let your dog lick him on the mouth.

He says the condoms are his roommate's— but he lives alone.

He is missing more than six teeth.

He says he loves and misses his kids but has no contact with them.

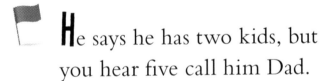 **H**e says he makes more or less money than he does.

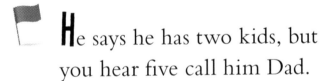 **H**e says he has two kids, but you hear five call him Dad.

He has photos of people he met yesterday but can't remember where.

He says he has never been married but has a wedding album.

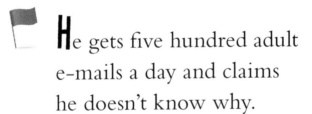

He can't remember his e-mail password when you're around.

He gets five hundred adult e-mails a day and claims he doesn't know why.

He always takes his
phone calls outside.

He has the address to several
correctional facilities …
but doesn't work for
law enforcement.

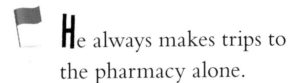

He claims to be drug free but has to take the little blue pills.

He always makes trips to the pharmacy alone.

He says he has never
looked at porn.

He asks you to marry him
during a collect call from jail.

He has more covered-up tattoos than actual tattoos.

He changes his religion to yours without any questions.

He says he has "quit"
his last seven jobs.

He pulls $100 from an
ATM at a gas station at 4:00
a.m. to buy you a gift …
from the gas station.

You find a strange ring in his hotel room; he claims it's a five-cent O-ring but insists on keeping it.

His shirts are tighter than yours.

You find crime scene tape in his garbage can.

He hides female names under male names on his phone.

He claims to have taken responsibility for all the debt in his divorce but never pays any bills.

He uses the company gas card to fill your car with gas.

He eyes your jewelry box more than once a day.

He says (with a straight face) he has a bionic arm with special powers.

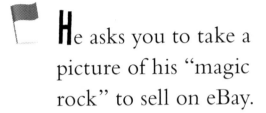 He asks you to take a picture of his "magic rock" to sell on eBay.

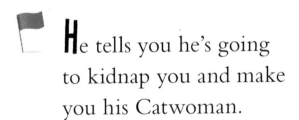 He tells you he's going to kidnap you and make you his Catwoman.

He tells you he loves you on your first date.

He lives with a female roommate who walks around in her underwear.

He says he has no social life, but there are 1,295 pictures of him with friends and in clubs on Facebook.

He says he will wait to have sex but makes serious moves on you on the first date.

He says his clothes are wet so he needs to take them off and put them in your dryer.

He says he's single—and then you find his and his wife's current insurance policy.

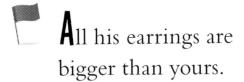 **A**ll his earrings are bigger than yours.

 He has the number sixty-nine in his screen name.

"Lady Killer" is his screen name.

He sends you a selfie—and it's a mug shot.

His profile picture
is from 1973.

He says he's thirty-two, but
kids call him Grandpa.

He freaks out if you talk to any of his friends.

His profile photo is from a security camera.

You can never go to his place.

His underwear is
prettier than yours.

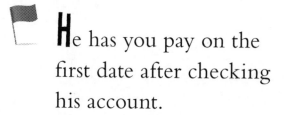

He has you pay on the first date after checking his account.

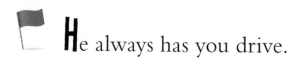

He always has you drive.

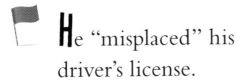

He pretends to drop something every time you pass a cop.

He "misplaced" his driver's license.

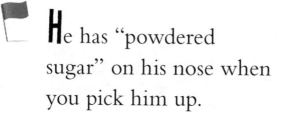 **H**e has "powdered sugar" on his nose when you pick him up.

 He has pictures of wedding rings on his phone, and you just met.

33

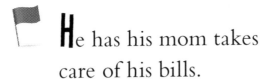 **H**e has his mommy come get his stuff after a breakup.

He has his mom takes care of his bills.

He says he does
everything alone.

He says good morning to his
truck before saying it to you.

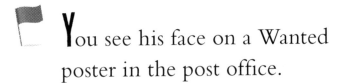

He has more pet names for his truck than you.

You see his face on a Wanted poster in the post office.

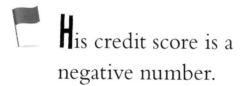

He gets lots of mail from the IRS, but he doesn't work for them.

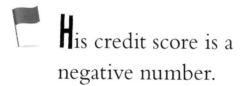

His credit score is a negative number.

He brags about fistfights at age fifty.

He refers to himself in the third person.

He uses his middle finger to wave at people.

He refers to himself by his video game character.

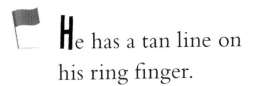 He has nude photos of himself on his cell phone.

He has a tan line on his ring finger.

He says he is looking for "normal," but his first question after exchanging numbers is your political view on the price of rice in China since the aliens took over.

His first line is, "I'm not like other men."

He takes you to a "clothing–optional" place on your first date.

He says he hates dogs, and you have four.

He says the bulky bracelet on his ankle is a fashion statement.

He has the word *Lucky* tattooed above his ... unit.

He texts you fifty times a day. (My girlfriends called this a Stage-Five Clinger.)

He feels guilty for missing his and his ex-wife's anniversary.

He says he has had
nineteen concussions.

He asks what you are wearing
before he asks your name.

You meet him in the women's underwear section at Wal-Mart.

You give him the wrong address to your place, and he still shows up.

He claims to be divorced; however, his wife is not aware of the fact.

You have to ask him if he has *your* jeans on.

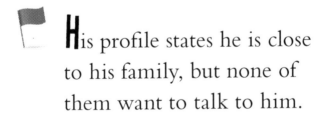

The first time you talk, he admits to being hung over from drinking an entire bottle of tequila the night before.

His profile states he is close to his family, but none of them want to talk to him.

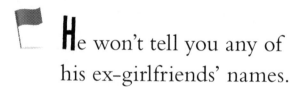 **H**e gets a phone call from his sister—and he doesn't have a sister.

He won't tell you any of his ex-girlfriends' names.

You find a hotel key card in his bag.

 He asks to put credit purchases under your name.

The words *bipolar, creep,* and *gigolo* come to mind when you first meet.

He has more bling on his hat than you have on your entire body.

51

He calls his mother more
than he calls you.

He owns three chihuahuas,
and they have more
clothes than you.

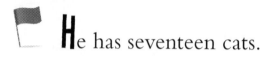

He has seventeen cats.

He won't interact with your children.

His profile only lists physical attributes of any woman he is looking to date.

He follows you around Wal-Mart and then tells you that you have lovely feet.

He's had more plastic surgery than Joan Rivers.

You find yourself constantly making excuses for him.

He sprays disinfectant spray everywhere you sit after you get up.

He refuses to give you his full name.

His screen name is Herpes Guy.

He won't send you a picture of himself.

ALONE

Humans weren't meant to be alone. Back in the day, I am sure, Adam sent God a text and told him he was lonely and bored. God didn't send him a NASCAR track or a PlayStation, he sent him a woman.

I have received a lot of unsolicited advice. In all reality, no one has been through exactly what we as individuals have been through in our lives. Some of us may experience a similar situation, but we are all unique. Our life experiences have molded us and will continue to mold us into the people we are today. Just as every fingerprint is different, each person's soul is different. No one knows your heart. No one knows exactly what you need. Sometimes even we ourselves are not sure what we need at any given moment.

I have been told to harden my heart. I can't do it. I have actually tried to harden my heart or be coldhearted. I feel that hardening your heart or seeking revenge is a waste of time and energy and has no positive outcome. What I *can* do is protect it with a shield. If more people had softer hearts, there would not be so much bitterness, revenge, and spitefulness. You *can* have a big heart. Just don't have a foolish heart.

Don't be afraid to be on your own. Sometimes we have to experience loneliness to appreciate companionship. I have always had a dog or two or four with me. I have never been truly alone.

I feel there is a difference between being single and being alone. No one wants to be alone.

When I get together with my parents for lunch or a gathering, they often say, "You talk a lot." I once again explain to them that as a dog groomer, I work with dogs all day. At home, I live with four dogs (which may call for another book?). I remind my parents that they get to talk to each other daily or argue whatever it is that married couples do these days. We all need human interaction or we just get ... weird. There are so many advantages to keeping a pet, particularly a dog. Don't get me wrong—I love cats, although I may have encouraged throwing things at your neighbor's earlier. Pets, particularly cats and dogs, have an amazing list of physical health benefits like lowering blood pressure, improving cardiovascular health, reducing risk of stroke, helping immune systems, and inspiring fitness through physical interaction. Just as important are the physiological benefits. Pets can reduce stress, decrease chances of suicide, help with social skills, calm nerves, offer comfort, and increase responsibility.

For me, my dogs provide comfort and protection. A dog's sense of smell and hearing are far better than ours. In fact, a dog's sense of smell is between one thousand and ten thousand times better than a human's. I rely on my dogs to let me know when someone, invited or not, is at my door. I rely on their protection when walking, hiking, or traveling. Their noses always tell me when a client's dog has escaped from the doggie salon in my home before I have had a chance to catch them.

I have been lucky to have a career I have a passion for. To be a dog groomer, you must have patience and a sense of humor. To be married, you must have patience and a sense of humor. Being happy in your career really affects your home life and health and stress levels. Three out of four of my dogs have been trained as forensic K-9s, so I have become in tune with their body language. I have also learned to discern "the printer downstairs just clicked off" from "the burglar is invading my home" barks. They are still learning that it's okay if the printer wants to shut off at 3:00 a.m.

IT MIGHT BE A RED FLAG IF...

Now I certainly do not recommend everyone throws out or forgoes an alarm system or whatever is needed to protect you and your family. I just call mine the Redneck Alarm System.

Besides being protectors, my dogs have become my companions in times of doubt or sadness. There have been times where my poor pups have had to endure hours of my crying and tears soaking their fur while I held them for comfort and reassurance. I know if they could talk during a crying episode, they would surely tell me no man is worth that amount of tears—so let's make some bacon!

There have been times when they have stood protectively in front of me during a verbal altercation. My seventeen-year-old Border Collie used to bare her teeth if someone hugged me, and we would have to be careful when someone playfully slugged me in the arm because she would jump up and nip at the person—never hard, but enough to let him or her know the dog was uncomfortable. Now she can't hear or see too well, so her protectiveness has lessened.

Nevertheless, she kept me from jumping off a cliff because I knew she would jump off that same cliff.

There have been many times I felt as if my dogs have been there for me when no one else was. They give love unconditionally, and it's nice to never have to come home to an empty house. Times when the garbage has been strewn throughout the house or my favorite pair of panties mysteriously disappeared have made me occasionally wonder if they're worth it … but they are.

There was a time when the above-mentioned Border Collie nipped at my ex husbands pants as he was leaving the yard. You know, I didn't really feel too bad until I heard my young daughter talking to him on the phone later that day, and I heard her say, "Your pants tore, Dad? Well, Mom gave her a treat after!"

I have been a single mom for most of my mothering years, and it can be done successfully. I started as a young bride at age eighteen.

I gave up a college scholarship and became a mother two weeks after turning nineteen. I was single by twenty and went through a messy divorce—so messy was the divorce that I still have an entire huge plastic tote with all the court documents and logbooks full of stories. I married again a few years later with no guidance and found myself single again at age thirty-one.

No, I wasn't a perfect mom, but my two children were safe and loved. They had clothes and food and the same opportunities kids with a two-parent household have. Yes, I believe a two-parent household is the best option for our children, but an unhealthy relationship can be detrimental to them. Even an unhealthy dating relationship can affect our children. When we have a negative experience, our children become involved whether we intentionally involve them or not. Being an example to our children has more merit than it is ever given credit for. Never endanger your children. Their future depends on your choices while they're under your care.

I feel very strongly about being an example, and although I have not been perfect, I have never skipped certain precautions when it came to the safety of my children. If it doesn't start with us teaching them right from wrong, it will never start. This is one of the reasons for this book.

Dating with children is a whole different ball game, and it is a tough game to play. When my daughters didn't approve of a man I'd met, they would send a dog into the living room with my underwear on its head. I have found that kids and dogs have very good judgment when it comes to adults.

Being alone can be one of the healthiest things we can do for ourselves. It gives us time to heal, reflect, and discover things about ourselves. Find all the positive things about living alone or at least being single. Focus on the positive and the things you enjoy. Find comfort in books, nature, pets, exercise, talking to a friend, finding inspiring quotes and write them down, or eating chocolate if you must. I often find I *must* eat chocolate. Help someone else in need, or listen to music that makes you happy. Everyone has his or her own taste in music. As a singer, music plays a big part in my life. I listen to my favorites and turn the volume up to drown out negative thoughts. I listen to Christian music and sing along when I really need it.

Do whatever it takes to make you feel comfortable and at peace. If you believe in a higher power, reach out for strength and serenity. I would not suggest shopping unless you have a lot of self-control. If not, the next thing you know, you find yourself on the next episode of *Hoarders*.

While being alone can be really self-empowering, there are a few situations where it can totally suck. For example, have you ever tried to get a soaking wet sports bra off? It's impossible to do alone; you either have to cut it off, pull a muscle attempting to get it off, or wear it for the rest of your life! Or when you pull off an award-winning karate move because you almost stepped on a spider and there is no one there to admire that particular move. I have invented several moves and have been known to walk on air with confronted by certain species of spiders. I have assaulted my own self when there has been a spider on me. My neighbors don't even look up anymore if I scream while outside; they have learned it's either a spider or dog poop.

I don't want to depend on others to build me up and tell me what qualities I have. I need to believe in myself and remind myself that I have worth, and my qualities make me who I am. A favorite quote of mine says, "The woman who does not require validation from anyone is the most feared person on the planet."

One of the most helpful things I do when going through a bout of depression or self-pity is write notes to myself to hang on my bathroom mirror that remind me of every positive attribute I have. I hang them in my master bathroom to see every morning when I look in the mirror. The mirror only shows us the outside of ourselves, but the notes help remind us what is on the inside. If only more mirrors were like that. They only show us our outward reflection, which we are often critical of, instead of a reflection of our inner beings.

One time I had written myself about twenty little notes and taped them to my mirror. My oldest daughter came to visit and happened to go into my bathroom when I wasn't expecting her to. I felt such embarrassment that she would see my silly little notes with my complete admission of self-doubt plastered across the mirror. Later that night, I went into my bathroom to not only find the notes I had written but at least fifteen others that she had written and taped on the mirror. It brought me to tears to know my own children could see the good in me while I struggled to see it.

What an inspiration that became. I knew that if my children felt that way about me, I was going to do my best not to disappoint them. It's a true gift when one or all of your children can remember the examples you set and still set for them. Of course my oldest still reminds me of her negative memories, like when I threw her beanie babies in the trash after she was told not to take them to school. I still feel bad! Even if we have set bad examples for our children, it is not too late. The beauty of human nature is that we are capable of change.

EXCUSES

People ask, "Why did you pick him?," or "Why did you take him back?," or "Why do you stay with him?" We all have reasons. Some say because they love him. Some even admit to being foolish. There are many different reasons we choose, and choose is the keyword to stay or keep pursuing someone who exhibits red flags.

My ignorance of red flags came from lack of self-confidence. I was bullied all through junior high and high school. Back then the awareness wasn't so prominent; we just called it "being mean." I was made to feel unworthy of compliments, incapable of being athletic, not popular enough for the "cool kids," called names in the hall, and had nasty notes stuffed in my locker.

Bullying can come from one person or several. When I was a student we had no systems or programs in place in school to help with this problem, which has been going on for centuries. I never had the courage to stand up for myself or not have the courage to let a single bully keep me from pursuing my interests at such a young age.

To this day it is something I struggle with, because society has set a preconceived standard that our looks, job, family, and relationships should be perfect. Young and old alike still feel like they need to adhere to the ideals we find in magazines or on TV shows. Most of the reality shows are not even reality. They have situations and dialog just like on sitcoms and dramas. The first time I discovered one of my favorite reality shows wasn't "real life," I was so mad. I saw the woman mouth the words that were written for her, and I found myself yelling at the TV (it happens). How can they call it reality if reactions are made up by the writers?

Okay, back to the subject. What I was cleverly leading into was that we are in control of our actions and reactions. Instead of working the issue out or coming up with a solution, I shrank. I didn't try out for the sports teams like I wanted. I didn't try out for cheerleader like I wanted. Everyone doesn't have to be an athlete or a cheerleader, but the bottom line was I didn't push and become what I wanted to be.

Looking back at those junior and high school days, making the cheer team wasn't life or death. But back then it felt like it was. Without even trying, I let someone else determine what I could or couldn't do, even though I was completely capable of doing it.

For a long time I thought a unicorn sliding down a rainbow to save me would make all my problems go away. I actually started writing what I thought back then was a book. I thought life was so unfair and that I was terribly picked on. I thought that someday young women would read that story and not allow themselves to be bullied or not allow themselves to be a bully.

As I got older, I thought help would come from a man who would save me and lift me up. Don't laugh, but I envisioned that I would meet my future husband at a roller-skating rink, and we would skate in slow motion to a song by Air Supply. Like most teenagers, I already had him picked out in high school. This particular boy was tragically killed our first year of high school. It's not until we realize that being saved and lifted up comes from within ourselves and with the help of God.

Childhood and teenage years are such an important time and can have a serious effect on adulthood, as it did mine. I was put on antidepressants in high school and have struggled to get off them ever since. Depression is not something to be ashamed of. Nearly 11 percent of Americans are on antidepressants, and more women than men use them.

Life gives us unexpected challenges. I never thought I would be told I could not have more children after my first daughter was born. It hit me like a ton of bricks. I clearly remember the minute I got the phone call; I was headed to give a seminar to youth about being bullied and being a bully. That was a difficult seminar to get through because I kept asking, "Why me?"

Those of you who have been paying attention will question my statement about having two daughters. I was lucky enough to adopt my second daughter when she was four years old. That adoption alone was not without trials and heartbreak. I couldn't prevent being cheated on during a marriage. I couldn't have prevented being laid off from my job while I was a single parent. I couldn't prevent the near loss of my child's life from a poor decision on her part. I couldn't prevent learning that my child was gay the night before her college graduation.

There are a lot of things we can't prevent, but we can be prepared and learn from everything that happens. Allow those things to make you stronger and wiser instead of bitter, cold, and untrusting. You deserve to be happy now. Whatever has happened is in the past, and that's why it is called the past. The past is something you cannot change, but you can change your future by your actions today. The problem comes when we allow someone or something to hurt us again. We often can't prevent hurt or at times can't see it coming, but there is no excuse for allowing ourselves to be hurt.

Often we sugarcoat an existing relationship. Of course we should always look for the good in people and concentrate on their strengths. The problem comes when we ignore the red flags because we make excuses for bad behavior or he manipulates us into thinking we caused that behavior. Everyone is in charge of her own behavior. (Easier said than done at times, I know.)

I had a conversation with a good friend about a particular relationship I was in. Sometimes it is wise to get advice from reliable, unbiased people in our lives. This is how the conversation went:

Her: "He cheated on you."

Me: "But he loves my dogs."

Her: "He lied to you."

Me: "But he makes me breakfast in bed."

Her: "He took advantage of your big heart."

Me: "But he thinks I'm sexy."

If you have ever had a conversation like that with someone, it's time to sit down and make a list of the positive and negative aspects of your relationship and focus on your priorities.

JENNIFER LOPEZ

The minute you start to wonder if you deserve better ... you do. A man or a woman can be a lot of things we like and are looking for, but when it comes to trust, respect, and integrity, nothing should overpower simple values.

FIGHT BACK

As adults, we still let someone else determine what we can or can't do, even though we may be completely capable of doing it. The only person standing in your way of doing anything you want in life is you.

First of all, we need to protect ourselves. I would love for background checks to be available to everyone and just might start a movement. It's okay for our employer to perform a background check on us, so why wouldn't and shouldn't we perform the same check on the person we are choosing to let into our hearts and homes? There are constant news stories about a woman who was murdered or abused by her husband or boyfriend. There are stories of men abusing or murdering a girlfriend's child.

Just recently I read about a woman who had been murdered by her boyfriend, who had been convicted of the murder of a girlfriend twenty years prior. Had the current girlfriend known his history, she might be alive today.

Another story was of a young boy who was being beaten by his mother's boyfriend, who had a record of abuse.

I just watched a well-known woman on the *Dr. Phil* show admit that two of her five boyfriends had been convicted of sexual abuse and all five had spent time in jail for one crime or another.

We run a Car Fax report on a car before we purchase it to check its history. When selling a home, the seller is required to disclose any problems the home has had or currently has. Why the heck shouldn't we do the same before we date or marry someone?

I know people make mistakes, but when a red flag is slapping you in the face, don't ignore it! There are small red flags and giant, raging red flags that, if we are in tune with our intuition more than our hearts, we can see. If there is something that just doesn't feel right, trust that feeling.

One of my favorite quotes is, "Don't ever forget your worth. The moment you accept less than your worth, you will get less. The moment you tolerate disrespect and disregard, you set a precedent."

If only more people had stronger faith in themselves. No one has the right to hurt you physically or emotionally. By tolerating abuse, we only weaken ourselves and give more power to the abuser. Even if you have ignored several flags, it's never too late.

If you have children, think about the example you are setting by allowing yourself to be abused, or lowering your standards because you don't want to be alone. Most importantly, *no one* is worth taking your own life or the life of another for. They say love is the most powerful emotion in the world. It is very easy to get tangled up in a situation where you are in danger or you have put your children's lives in danger. It's never too late to get out of a relationship or situation you have gotten yourself into. There is always help; there are programs to use and places to go.

It's so easy to play the blame game. Sometimes we think that when certain things turn out the way they do, it is all part of God's plan for us. I am a true believer that all things happen for a reason. Sometimes we do not immediately know the reason they happened. There is a saying: "God doesn't give us more than we can handle." Sometimes I look upward and say,

"Are you serious? Are you trying to kill me? Give me a break, please!"

You can't change what has happened or what is supposed to happen. Your best defense is your free agency, which stares you in the face and asks, "What next?" It is so easy to make an excuse for any decision you make. It's easy to blame someone else, a condition, the past, or a weakness. Then you have to blame someone or something for that weakness or past or condition, and it becomes an endless cycle that is so self-destructive it sneaks up on us without us knowing. Many times we are responsible for our own decisions that end up leaving us hurt and scarred. Then who do we blame? When we start blaming ourselves, we start doubting ourselves.

Ultimately it is not about blaming anyone or anything. It's about having the strength to deal with life as it is dealt to you and choosing how you will react. No one is perfect. If we would spend more time worrying about our own small imperfections that can be changed and less about others, this world would be a much happier place.

There will always be mean people in this world, and there will always be men who will say everything you want to hear because they know you will stay with them or tolerate their abuse. I have met men who would argue with God himself and try to talk a car salesman out of his own car.

The key with men like that is to not depend or make decisions based on things they say; you base your feelings and actions on their actions, good or bad. Don't ever let anyone make you feel bad for standing up for yourself and protecting your heart. One of my most comforting quotes is from inspirational speaker Nadia T: "A strong woman does not define herself by what others say, she defines herself by the truest measure of a good woman; the creator himself knows her intentions and sees her true heart."

This is for all the women out there with true hearts who just haven't believed enough in themselves to see it. Once you see it, everyone else will. Those who don't see it need to go back to the drawing board and take a good look at themselves.

You are strong, you are beautiful, and you are one of a kind.

ABOUT THE AUTHOR

Jennifer Lopez was born in Oregon and has spent most of her life in a small town in Utah. Jennifer grew up singing, dancing, acting, and bringing home every stray animal she could find. Jennifer attended the College of Eastern Utah in Price, Utah on a music scholarship soon after becoming a mother to a beautiful daughter. Ten years later, Jennifer was able to adopt her second daughter. Jennifer turned her attention to training and handling dogs and became a forensic K-9 handler for a local law enforcement agency. She has received several awards for her volunteer work with the K-9's. That title has allowed her to travel to several states, working with law enforcement agencies, including the FBI. Jennifer currently owns a dog grooming salon and works with dogs outside her home. Jennifer also sings locally and throughout the state. She currently lives in Helper, Utah with her four dogs.